Elsmere Library
30 Spruce Avenue
Wilmington, DE 19805

NO LONGER THE
PROPERTY OF
NEW CASTLE COUNTY

NO LONGER
THE
PROPERTY

Ripley's WILD ANIMALS

Believe It or Not!®

Mason Crest Publishers

Written by Camilla de la Bedoyere
Consultant Barbara Taylor

Originally published by

PUBLISHING

Publisher Anne Marshall

Managing Editor Rebecca Miles
Picture Researcher James Proud
Editors Lisa Regan, Rosie Alexander
Assistant Editor Amy Harrison
Proofreader Judy Barratt
Indexer Hilary Bird

Art Director Sam South
Design Rocket Design (East Anglia) Ltd
Reprographics Stephan Davis

www.masoncrest.com

Copyright © 2011 by Mason Crest Publishers. All rights reserved. No part of this publication may be reproduced or transmitted in any form or by any means, electronic or mechanical, including photocopying, recording, taping,or any information storage and retrieval system, without permission from the publisher.

ISBN 978-1-4222-1835-8 (hardcover)

ISBN 978-1-4222-2073-3 (ppk)

Series ISBN (8 titles): 978-1-4222-1827-3

10 9 8 7 6 5 4 3 2 1

For information regarding permission, write to VP Intellectual Property, Ripley Entertainment Inc., Suite 188, 7576 Kingspointe Parkway, Orlando, Florida 32819 e-mail: publishing@ripleys.com

Library of Congress Cataloging-in-Publication Data is available.

Printed in USA

PUBLISHER'S NOTE
While every effort has been made to verify the accuracy of the entries in this book, the Publishers cannot be held responsible for any errors contained in the work. They would be glad to receive any information from readers.

WARNING
Some of the stunts and activities in this book are undertaken by experts and should not be attempted by anyone without adequate training and supervision.

CONTENTS

PAGE 9

PAGE 14

TWISTS

ALL CREATURES GREAT AND SMALL

WORLDWIDE WONDERS

WHAT'S INSIDE YOUR BOOK!

TWISTS

Aren't animals amazing? From tiny terrors to gentle giants, vicious predators to graceful grazers, our planet is home to over one million different species. Each one of these species has an important role to play in the way the world works. That's why it's so vital that we consider how our lifestyles affect the homes and habitats of every living creature today.

This book will open your eyes to the truly astonishing, the fearsomely frightening, and even the fantastically freakish members of the animal kingdom. Find out more about ocean dwellers, microscopic marvels, and endangered creatures, with Ripley's fascinating facts and amazing "Believe It or Not!" stories from around the world. Come on—read all about it!

Only male lions have a mane of long hair around their face. The males defend the pride (group) of lions and their territory, but the females are in charge of hunting and bringing home supper for the whole pride.

KEY FACTS

- A pride may cover up to 100 square miles as its territory.
- Lions learn to hunt when they are about a year old.
- A lion has a claw at the back of its leg, which it sometimes uses to pick leftovers from its teeth.
- The back teeth are used for cutting meat (rather than grinding food, like many other animals).

Do the twist

This book is packed with incredible creatures. It will teach you amazing things about wild animals, but like all Twists books, it shines a spotlight on things that are unbelievable but true. Turn the pages and find out more...

Twists are all about Believe It or Not: amazing facts, feats, and things that will make you go "Wow!".

Found a new word? Big word alerts will explain it for you.

Believe It or Not!®

The animal kingdom is full of creatures that sound like they're made up, but they're totally for real. Like this two-headed turtle, which has two heads, a pair of front feet on each side, one pair of back legs, and one tail. It's actually conjoined twins, and is on display in an aquarium in Pennsylvania.

FAMILY MATTERS

GETTING TOGETHER

The multi-colored peacock is a bird that dresses to impress. He can fan out his tail, in an eye-opening display of shimmering colors and stunning patterns.

...s an ingenious tactic; a show-off with ...fect plumage is more likely to attract ... attention of the watching peahens. ...males admire bright colors and large ...pots" in the feathers—and the more

eyespots the better! Once a female has chosen her favorite male she will mate with him, and soon starts laying eggs. The most marvelous males win over a number of females to mate with, while shabby-looking peacocks remain alone.

BIG WORD ALERT

REPRODUCTION
The way that an animal has young is called reproduction. Some animals can have young all by themselves, but it's more common to have two parents: a male and a female.

LIFE STORIES

The story of how an animal lives, from birth to death, is a life-cycle.

If an animal can find a healthy and strong mate it is more likely to have young that will survive. Some animals make a big effort to impress those they fancy—to show how fit they are. This is called a courtship.

Mammals are animals that give birth to live young and feed them with milk. Usually it's the mom who provides the milk, but in the job-sharing world of Dayak fruit bats, it's a job for the dads too!

You said we were friends!
During mating, a female praying mantis usually gets the munchies and bites off her partner's head!

twist it!

A queen white ant, or termite, lays 30,000 eggs a day!

Snakes and lizards are reptiles and lay their eggs on land.

Amphibians, such as frogs and toads, have to lay their eggs in water, and males will fight each other, sometimes to the death, to mate with them.

Female rhinos spray smelly urine, them until they hatch.

male's body, and he takes care of eggs inside a special pouch on the for each other every day during the mating period. The female lays her

Sea horses are romantic, dancing

TRUE LOVE

DADDY DAY-CARE
Male jawfish protect their eggs by keeping them inside their enormous mouths. Without their fatherly care, chances are that most of the eggs would be eaten before ever hatching.

Look for the Ripley R to find out even more than you knew before!

Learn fab fast facts to go with the cool pictures.

Don't forget to look out for the "twist it!" column on some pages. Twist the book to find out more fast facts about amazing animals.

31

If you are equipped with killer claws, razor-sharp teeth, or toxic venom you could be a perfect predator—an animal that hunts to eat.

Which predator would you place at the top of the list of mean, keen, killing machines? Sharks are a favorite for first place—after all, they've been prowling the oceans for around 400 million years. That means they were slicing through flesh 200 million years before the dinosaurs started plodding around on land! So are these hungry hunters the world's top predators? Since people kill around 100 million sharks every year—driving many types to the edge of extinction—that top spot might actually belong to us shame-faced humans.

The alligator snapping turtle catches fish when they seize its tongue, which they mistake for a worm.

PREDATORS
Animals that kill and eat other animals. The animals they kill are called prey.

BIG WORD ALERT

Tiger sharks attack almost anything, including people. One was found with cans, tires, wood, half a dead dog, and a tom-tom drum in its belly!

Open wide
The Great White shark attacks ferociously, then retreats, letting the damaged prey grow weaker. Then it returns to finish it off. Each year, 50 to 100 serious shark attacks are reported, with an average of less than ten deaths.

THE FROG THAT FOUGHT BACK!

When this little tree frog got attacked by a cat-eyed snake he decided he wasn't going to give up without a fight. He grabbed hold of the snake's neck, and the predator and prey were still locked in mortal combat three hours later!

Just one bite!

In 1963, spearfishing champion Rodney Fox was attacked by a Great White shark in the ocean off Aldinga Beach, Australia. He had been virtually bitten in half and required 462 stitches. Less than three months later, however, he was back in the water, carrying a reminder of the attack embedded in his hand: a Great White tooth.

Knockout!

Mantis shrimps are a knockout! These crustaceans have the fastest and most powerful punch in the animal kingdom. They can pound their prey with a force of 1,000 newtons—that's as deadly as a rifle bullet, and strong enough to smash glass. The shrimp's weapons are a pair of club-shaped legs that are tucked away under its head, until the time comes to lash out at a super-ballistic speed of up to 790 feet/second!

TINY TERROR

When it is worried, the blue-ringed octopus buzzes with color. Its blue ring markings pulse brightly and its brown skin turns a vivid yellow. It measures only about 8 inches from armtip to armtip, but it has a deadly bite, which contains enough venom to kill at least seven people. In 1967, a man paddling in an Australian rock pool lived for just 90 minutes after being bitten.

A shrimp's weapons of smash destruction are folded under its head until it's time for lunch.

TAKE A DIVE

DEEP DWELLERS

Oceans teem with animal life, from crystal-clear waters around coral reefs, to their darkest, inky depths. This may be where life on Earth began—simple creatures were burrowing in the slime of the ocean floor an unbelievable one billion years ago!

Oceans and seas are a mighty food store, and home to all sorts of creatures, from enormous blue whales with an average length of 90 feet, to tiny rotifers—each one smaller than a grain of salt. From the shallow shore to the deep ocean trenches, more than 6 miles beneath the surface, animals are crawling, slithering, tunneling, swimming, floating, and drifting.

When the tiny male anglerfish mates, he grabs the larger female with his mouth, hangs on, and gradually fuses (joins) with her body.

In the vast, black ocean depths it can take time to find a breeding partner. The male deep-sea anglerfish becomes a part of the female. He shares her food via her blood supply, and in return fertilizes her eggs.

Most of the male body disintegrates (his eyes, nostrils, everything) apart from what is needed to fertilize the female's eggs. Once this takes place, the male can never leave.

PHYTOPLANKTON

The oceans are packed with phytoplankton (say: fie-toe-plank-ton). These mini plants get energy from sunlight, and are the favorite food of billions of animals.

BIG WORD ALERT

WAY DOWN

Fish were the first animals with backbones to evolve on Earth and there are more than 30,000 species, or different types, of fish. Most of them live in the oceans or seas.

A shark's skeleton isn't made of bone, it's made of cartilage. That's the soft stuff you have holding your nose together. There are around 500 species of shark, of which only about 40 occasionally attack people.

Clownfish seek safety in the stinging tentacles of sea-anemones. The fish are immune to the stings, and clean the anemone in return for a safe place to live.

If you spot puffer fish on a menu, don't order it! Although these fish are sometimes served in Japanese restaurants, they contain enough poison to kill a person in 20 minutes. Chefs have to train for years to learn how to remove all the deadly body parts. Would you risk it?

Coral reefs are ocean wildlife hotspots. They are formed from living creatures, called coral polyps, and are home to thousands of other types of water species. Many coral reefs are dying, due to pollution and human activity.

twist it!

This red handfish looks grumpy! Maybe that's because he has to get around by walking on his "hands," which are really just fins.

Many ocean-going creatures crunch on krill. These little animals swim in giant groups called swarms.

Oceans and seas are salty, but rivers and lakes have much less salt in the water. Animals usually live in one or the other habitat, but rarely both.

Ripley's Believe It or Not!®

Slithering sea slugs lost their shells millions of years ago. They don't need them, because these soft-bodied creatures have toxins (poisons) and stinging cells in their skin. Their bright colors are a bold signal to keep clear, or prepare for pain!

YIKES!

Deep in the oceans, where sunlight never reaches, there's a small army of weird creatures. Deep-water fish, such as this vicious viperfish, usually have dark bodies, huge mouths and hundreds of light organs called photophores. These are parts of the body that can actually make light, helping the fish to find food in the murky depths. The viperfish's teeth protrude far beyond its mouth and eyes, giving it the longest teeth of any animal (in proportion to its head). If your teeth were this big, they would stick out a ridiculous 12 inches!

Most animals that live in the seas and oceans are able to take oxygen from the water. Don't try this in the bathtub: we're equipped with air-breathing lungs, not gills.

If you were an animal, would you choose to crawl like a caterpillar or fly like a moth? Flying wins every time—can you imagine the thrill of swooping and soaring through the air?

Only birds, bats, and insects use their own mighty muscle power to truly fly. That little problem hasn't put off other creatures, such as flying squirrels and frogs, from taking a brave leap and trusting the wind to carry them along. Gliding is great if you're lazy, but animals that soar through the air can't always control how they travel, and where they end up. So it's fingers crossed for a soft landing!

Eagle-eyed ospreys soar over water looking for fish. They plunge, feet first, and grab their prey with talons that are covered in slippery-fish gripping spikes. They can even close their nostrils when they dive, so they don't get water up their nose.

KEY FACTS

- Flying can be a great way to get beyond the reach of predators. Plus, while you're flying past that tree, you might just spot some juicy fruits to eat too...

- ...which is just as well, because flying is hard work. It takes a great deal of energy—flying animals have big appetites.

- A bird's flapping wings create an up-force, which lifts the animal into the sky.

A HEAD FOR HEIGHTS

FLYERS

It flies, it hums, and it sips nectar.

Is it a hummingbird? No, this is a hummingbird hawk moth. When it flies, this insect's orange hindwings beat so fast they look like flickering flames, giving the impression that the moth is on fire.

Hummingbirds have trough-shaped tongues and long, skinny beaks. They work like a drinking straw—perfect for sipping sweet nectar and the occasional insect, too.

The heart of a ruby-throated hummingbird beats around 600 times a minute.

The hummingbird has the biggest heart and wings in proportion to body size of all warm-blooded animals!

Bats are the only mammals that can fly, rather than glide. Their wings are made from double layers of skin that stretch from fingers to ankles.

When a tropical two-wing flying fish needs to escape a predatory dolphin it flaps its enormous fins to gain liftoff, and sails out of the water and through the air for up to 40 seconds.

It's almost impossible to swat a fly—they move quickly, have great eyesight that allows them to see in virtually every direction, and can sense the air moving in front of your hand long before it reaches them.

Want to know the funny thing about flying lemurs? They can't really fly, and aren't really lemurs! These furry mammals live in Southeast Asia and have kite-shaped membranes of skin stretched between their limbs. They leap off trees, spread out the skin, and glide for up to 450 feet.

FLY BY

Wallace's flying frog is an amphibian with an ambition to fly! It may not have wings, but this animal has got wide webbed feet and skin flaps that catch the air. When a frog jumps from a tree it can glide for up to 50 feet.

wow!

>> HIGH-FLYERS >>

- Some bats chase moths to heights of 10,000 feet.
- Alpine choughs (a type of bird) fly at 30,000 feet in the Himalayas.
- Queen of Spain Fritillary butterflies have been found at 9,000 feet.

ON THE FAR SIDE

Animals have to cope with extremes of temperature and all sorts of difficult conditions. If you're thirsty, you get a glass of water. If you're cold, you put on more clothes. It's all about controlling what's going on inside, and outside, so your body can reach maximum performance levels. And that's what animals do, too.

FISH ON THE ROCKS

The blood of an icefish contains chemical antifreeze, which stops it from turning solid in the chilly waters of the Antarctic.

warm wallow

Japanese macaques make the most of the cold weather by enjoying a dip in the warm waters of a hot spring. They have even been known to make and throw snowballs, rolling them along the ground to get bigger and better ones!

BIG WORD ALERT

HABITAT
The place an animal lives. Some animals have evolved to be able to live in extreme habitats.

KEY FACTS

- It's worth being an extreme survivor if you can find safety or food in a place where few other animals venture.
- Animals living in very hot, cold, dry, or wet places often need super-adapted body parts.

BIG BULLY!

Frogs like it damp, so when there is no rain, large African bullfrogs bury themselves underground. They can survive for several years, wrapped in a cocoon so they don't dry out.

This African frog has seized its prey—a small mouse!

WHO'S THE COLDEST?

- Arctic foxes can survive at −22°F if well fed.

- Snow buntings nest nearer to the North Pole than any other bird.

- Ptarmigans can survive sub-zero temperatures for six weeks.

- Himalayan yaks survive at a height of 20,000 feet on ice-fields.

EXTREMES!

Less than ½ inch of rain falls in the Namibian Desert every year. Desert adders living there don't drink water; they get all they need from the lizards they eat.

Some animals sleep their way through the worst weather of winter. Little Siberian birch mice hibernate for up to eight months of the year.

Black grouse spend up to 95 percent of the winter hidden deep in snow burrows. The only time they emerge is to have a snack!

Musk oxen have been around since the Ice Age, and they still use thick woolen coats to keep them warm in Alaska. Their fur reaches to the ground, and is the longest growing hair of any animal.

Twist it!

Little baby ears are perfect for keeping in body heat.

Two layers of thick fur help to keep out the cold.

You won't see a polar bear putting on a coat! This extreme survivor has got a body that can cope with sub-zero temperatures. In fact, polar bears get too hot sometimes, and roll around in the snow to chill out! They are the largest predators on land.

REACHING THE MAX

Who's the biggest?

TALLEST GIRAFFE
19 feet 8 inches (in height)

BIGGEST DINOSAUR
Argentinosaurus
98 feet (in length)

LARGEST ON LAND
African elephant
35 feet (from trunk to tail)

BIGGEST EVER BLUE WHALE
110 feet (in length)

This enormous individual was a real giant amongst elephants. He was an African bush elephant and was shot in Angola in 1974. He measured 13 feet 8 inches to the shoulder and was thought to weigh 13.5 tons, which makes him about twice the length and weight of an average bull elephant. The elephant was stuffed and you can now see him in the Smithsonian Museum of Natural History, Washington DC, USA.

HORN OF PLENTY

FASCINATING FACT! FASCINATING FACT!

Lurch, an African Watusi steer, has horns that are 7 feet 6 inches across and 38 inches around... and they're still growing! His parents have perfectly normal horns.

Tallest animal!

The giraffe has a tongue almost 20 inches in length!

Millipedes have more legs than any other creature, but they don't actually have 1,000 of them. The most ever counted on one millipede was 750 legs.

Gaboon vipers have hollow teeth that pump venom into their victim. They have the longest fangs of any snake and one bite contains enough venom to kill ten people.

For its size, the rhino beetle is the strongest animal on the planet, and can move an object 850 times its own weight!

The world's biggest earthworms can grow to 16½ feet long, and are as thick as your arm. Bootlace worms, found in coastal areas of Britain, can measure 180 feet!

Deep in the oceans, whales talk to each other using grunting and moaning sounds. Some of these sounds are the loudest animal noises ever recorded. They are about as loud as a rocket taking off!

Spotted skunks stink...and that's official. They are the smelliest animals alive, and even perform headstands when they spray their foul liquids, to get the best results.

twist it!

BIG, REALLY BIG!

A colossal squid is a giant in anyone's book. This one turned up in the nets of a fishing boat in the Ross Sea, near Antarctica. It was the first intact specimen ever seen, measured around 33 feet in length, and had eyeballs bigger than dinner plates. They probably gave this creature great vision deep underwater, where very little light can penetrate.

The stripe leg tarantula devours a tasty lizard. It is one of the largest spiders in the world and lives in the Amazon area of South America.

ACTUAL SIZE!

OVERSIZE JUMPER

This goliath frog must be hopping mad he got caught! These bulky amphibians live in West Africa and can measure 16 inches from nose to tail.

TWIST IT!

Tiny tarsiers live in the rain forests of Southeast Asia. They spend most of their time scampering through trees, using their long, slender fingers to grip to branches. Tarsiers can turn their heads right around, to check what's going on behind them, and use their enormous eyes and excellent hearing to listen for prowling predators.

Little fennec foxes have enormous ears. They live in the desert and come out to hunt when the sun goes down. Their large ears help them to listen for prey, but they also help the foxes to lose heat during the boiling desert days.

A mole 6 inches long can dig a tunnel almost 230 feet long in a single night.

A solitary dingo (a species of Australian wild dog) can kill 50 sheep in one night.

Oilbirds spend their entire lives in darkness, inhabiting the caves of South America. They venture out at night to feed on fruit and find their way around using echolocation.

A barn owl, hearing a mouse, can take off in half a second, fly 12½ feet per second, and adjust its talons to the size and shape of its prey—in the dark!

The barn owl catches more mice than 12 cats!

An owl's eyes take up about half of the space in its head.

Watch this!

WHOO'S THERE?

NOCTURNAL HUNTERS

When the sun slips down in the sky, stealthy stalkers begin to stir. Millions of animals, from wolves to wombats, join the wide-awake club and get active under the cover of night.

On the up side, night workers should be hard to see, so they might avoid being eaten. The downer is that lots of other wide-awakers have got crafty methods for seeking out prey at night.

Suckers!

Blood-drinking vampire bats feed on other animals and, occasionally, humans too. Here they are feeding on a cow's foot, slicing through flesh, and sucking up the oozing blood. Chemicals in their spit stop the wound from healing.

Freaky frogmouths are peculiar-looking nocturnal birds. They perch near the ground, looking for insects and small animals to pounce upon and eat with their large mouths.

If a frogmouth is frightened it clings to a tree, stays still, and pretends to be a broken branch!

Ouch! Barn owls usually swallow their small prey whole. Creatures such as mice, birds, lizards, and frogs are eaten, feathers, bones, and all!

Ripley's Believe It or Not!®
Night beast

A strange hairless animal was found dead outside Cuero, Texas, in August 2007. It was thought to be a chupacabra, a mythical nocturnal beast. The chupacabra gets its name (Spanish for goat-sucker) from its habit of attacking and drinking the blood of livestock. Descriptions of a chupacabra vary: a hairless dog-like creature; a spiny reptile that hops and has red glowing eyes. As for this animal: some believed it was a fox with mange...or was it?

KEY FACTS

- Around half of all the animals that live on land are nocturnal. That means they head out and about at night, but sleep in the day.

- Nocturnal creatures often need super senses, so they can find their way around in the dark.

- Animals that live in hot places often stir at night, because it's easier to keep cool once the sun has set.

MIGHTY MUNCHERS

Feeling a bit empty inside? Are you hungry enough to eat 2,500 hamburgers? If you were a furry shrew, that's the same amount of food you'd have to find and eat every day of your life! Except it wouldn't be burgers you'd be eating, it would be nearly your own body weight in bugs, slugs, and grubs. Tasty!

YUK!

Spotted hyenas are the most powerful scavengers in the world with jaws and teeth that can exert enough pressure to smash rocks, and can crush, and then digest, bone, horn, hooves, and hides.

It's tough, but true: some animals need to eat all day long to stay alive. Consider a swarm of desert locusts: each insect weighs only 0.07 ounces, but when you've got 16,000,000,000 of them devouring any crops in their path, that's a jaw-dropping 35,000 tons of food every 24 hours.

really?

Big animals need lots of food. Most blue whales reach about 89 feet long and eat 2,200 pounds of krill every single day to survive. Krill are shrimp-like creatures, and each one is no bigger than your little finger!

Faddy diets are common in nature. Giant anteaters, for example, are fussy eaters that devour tens of thousands of ants and termites daily. They can't eat anything else. Vampire bats live on a diet of blood.

Some animals swallow food whole, others mash it with their teeth first. Flies, however, vomit burning juices on to their lunch before sucking it up like soup. Yum!

Ripley's Believe It or Not!®

One sandtiger shark in the "womb" kills and eats all of its brothers and sisters. A scientist was once dissecting a dead female sandtiger and had his finger bitten by the one surviving baby shark!

BIG WORD ALERT

OMNIVORE	– Eats anything
HERBIVORE	– Nature's vegetarians
CARNIVORE	– Mighty meat eater
PISCIVORE	– Loves a fish dinner

This 13-foot Burmese python bit off more than it could chew when it tried to swallow a 6-foot American alligator, whole. Both animals were found dead, floating in the water. Experts think the alligator was still alive when the snake swallowed it, snout-first, and that repeated kicks from its hind legs made a hole in the snake's stomach wall.

Snake's stomach.

Alligator's tail.

OPEN WIDE

Pets, like people, are getting bigger and unhealthier. Lack of exercise and over-feeding are causing pooches and pussycats to pile on the weight. The world's biggest domestic cats weigh as much as a five-year-old child!

The caterpillar of the polyphemus moth is a record-breaking mighty muncher. It eats 86,000 times its own birthweight in just 56 days. That's like a human baby eating 300 tons of food!

When Kyle, a small collie/Staffordshire bull terrier, got hungry, he swallowed a bread knife measuring 15 inches. Amazingly, Kyle survived his dangerous snack attack!

Dust mites make a meal from dead skin and hair. Millions can live in just an ounce of dust, causing asthma and other allergic symptoms.

When a Nile crocodile was killed in 1968, its stomach was found to contain the remains of a woman, two goats, and half a donkey!

twist it!

SPEED MERCHANTS

In the nasty world of nature there's one golden rule to staying alive: run for it! Whether you're chasing lunch, or on the menu yourself, speed is a vital survival skill. When a pronghorn antelope smells the hot breath of a coyote nearby, it springs into action. Within just a few seconds, these graceful grazers turn into power-houses that can reach breathtaking speeds of 42 mph for a mile, making them the world's fastest long-distance runners. How do humans compare? Even the world's speediest sprinter can manage only a measly 23 mph for ten seconds.

A very flexible spine helps the cheetah make enormous strides.

BIG WORD ALERT

ACCELERATE
When an animal increases its speed it accelerates.

Grippy claws dig in to accelerate.

Whooooosh!

Cheetahs are the fastest land animals over a short distance. They can achieve top speeds thanks to their light and muscular bodies. Their spine is incredibly flexible, which means these big cats can take enormous strides. Their claws grip the ground as they run, just like the spikes on a human sprinter's running shoes.

>> WHO'S THE FASTEST? >>

Peregrine falcon
124 mph

Sailfish 68 mph

Cheetah 60 mph

Pronghorn 42 mph

Speed freaks

<< Killer crabs

Ghost crabs are crusty crustaceans with ten legs, two of which are claws. They live by the ocean, and burrow into soft sand along the beach. At night, they come out to feed (this one is about to snack on a dead turtle) but the slightest disturbance will send them racing back to their tunnels. Ghost crabs run sideways very fast and can cover over 6 feet in just one second.

Living torpedoes >>

All penguins are clumsy waddlers on land, but watch them in the ocean and their funny-looking bodies are perfect for being propelled through water. They have torpedo-shaped bodies and wings like flippers that cut through water, reducing water resistance. Gentoo penguins of the Antarctic region are the fastest of all.

KEY FACTS

- Speed: it's great for getting you out of trouble, but it takes a lot of energy, and a body that's built for rapid action.

- Being able to move fast is handy if you're a predator, as long as you can move quicker than your prey.

- If you belong to a speedy species you may find you become someone else's lunch when you can't move so fast. Most at risk are newborns, and injured or elderly animals.

- Speedy creatures need to eat plenty of food to replace all the energy they burn.

twist it!

Despite their huge and bulky bodies, elephants can thunder along the African plains at speeds of 15 mph.

Scientists at the University of Washington, USA, wanted to find out which reptile can move fastest, so they set up a racetrack! As the lizards raced they passed through light beams that triggered a timing device. The spiny-tailed iguana won the race, reaching an impressive 21 mph!

Animals on land can usually move more quickly, and easily, than animals under water. That's because water exerts a greater force (water resistance) than air. Peregrine falcons are the fastest animals of all when they fall into a dive because gravity helps them on their way.

Three-toed sloths prefer slo-mo. It would take them an hour to walk 400 feet, if they could be bothered!

A GOOD RUN

Man 23 mph   Iguana 21 mph   Elephant 15 mph   Sloth... 400 FEET per hour!

JOURNEYS

MIGRATION

DIAMOND RAYS

WHEN THOUSANDS OF GOLDEN RAYS SET OFF ON THEIR ANNUAL TRIP ALONG THE EASTERN COAST OF MEXICO, THEY TURN THE SEA INTO AN AWESOME DIAMOND-PATTERNED SPECTACLE. EACH FISH MEASURES UP TO 7 FEET ACROSS, AND SWIMS BY FLAPPING ITS ENORMOUS TRIANGULAR-SHAPED FINS LIKE WINGS.

WILDEBEEST VACATION

This is me!

Look mom, I can fly!

Turtles have been swimming through the oceans for 220 million years. But it's hard to find any of them, because they are always on the move!

These shelled reptiles are a blast from the past, and have a weird creature feature: they go on marathon journeys. When a newly hatched female loggerhead turtle emerges from her egg, she is just 2 inches long. She wades into the sea and begins a lonely journey that will take up to ten years and cover nearly 10,000 miles. The adult turtle then returns to the same place where she hatched, to lay her own clutch of eggs.

Sadly, my best friend Bob didn't make it.

Asking the lions for directions was not the best idea.

Ahhhh, the green, green, grass of home

When wily wildebeest travel they make a big deal of it, migrating for seven months in search of food. They follow the rains north, and can hear thunderstorms 20 miles away. They know that where there's rain there is juicy green grass. Yum!

get off the line!

COAST TRIP

Every year, 120 million red crabs crawl out of their burrows on Christmas Island and head to the coast. But this is no summertime spree... these brave crabs are marching off to mate. They have to make it past roads, railroads, and farms to reach the Indian Ocean.

MIGRATION

A long journey is called a migration. These incredible trips usually happen at certain times of the year, and often following the same routes. Animals migrate to get to more food, or to find a better place to mate. Many migrations happen from places that are cold in winter to ones that are warm in summer. It's a bit like going on vacation.

BIG WORD ALERT

UNDER THE LENS
MICROSCOPIC MARVELS

Get up close and personal with the hairy, scary side of nature. All you need is a microscope. All these creatures are magnified many times—scary!

KEY FACTS

- Microscopes magnify things, which means that they look bigger and you are able to see much more detail.
- Scientists can use Scanning Electron Microscopes (SEMs) to get amazing pictures of tiny things. SEMs can magnify something 250,000 times!
- Without microscopes we wouldn't know much about bacteria, viruses, and other tiny living creatures.

Ant

Journey to OUTER SPACE!

No, it's not an alien, but this ant's cousins have been to space. Fifteen ant astronauts were sent into space so scientists could see how they coped with life there. The ants went crazy, digging tunnels!

Wasp

This flying insect has a sting in the tail and a tough, hairy skin called an exoskeleton.

Sharks have rough skin and tooth-like scales, which are made from material similar to the white enamel on your teeth! The scales of most fish, however, are made of bone and are smooth and shiny.

Butterfly wing

When light hits the rows of tiny scales on this butterfly wing, the wing appears to turn a brilliant, shimmering blue.

Tapeworm

His nasty little hooks attach to the inside of your gut where he can absorb your juices!

Gecko

Wall-climbing geckos have lots of super-sticky hairs on their feet.

FASCINATING FACT

25

HOW CLEVER!

PROBLEM SOLVING

Imagine someone has put a wad of banknotes in a jar, and sealed it shut. If you can get the money out of the jar, it's yours. What would you do?

You'd quickly put your thinking cap on, of course! You use your brilliant brain to think up ways to tackle every problem you come across. That makes you one of the most intelligent animals on the planet, despite what your teachers might say! Maybe humans are the *most* intelligent species, but who knows? There are plenty of other clever creatures, and being a problem solver is a top survival skill in the competitive world of animals.

Hmmm, a bit more to the left...

Mother chimps show their youngsters how to do important jobs, like using a twig to catch termites. When one mother chimp realized her son was daydreaming, she gave him a slap to make him concentrate!

Brain boxes

- Intelligent animals usually have big brains, but it does depend on the size of the animal's body.

- Really clever creatures are able to learn how to do new tasks.

- It's difficult to figure out how intelligent animals are because you can't give them a written test. But you can give them problems to solve

Becky
Rosie
Jamie
Anne
Michelle
Charlotte
Samantha

HEY, I KNOW EWE
Sheep can recognize the faces of up to 50 other members of the flock!

JUMPING

SPITTING

Are you left- or right-handed? It's thought that octopuses also have a favorite "arm," though, of course, they have eight to choose from. Scientists have given them toys such as blocks, balls, and puzzles to see whether there is a pattern to how they pick them up.

FISH FOOD
An archerfish shoots a jet of water at its insect prey to knock it down and gobble it up. Adult archerfish usually hit their target with the first shot, and this can be up to 5 feet away. If the prey is close to the water, however, the fish will leap out to grab it with its mouth.

twist it!

Big baby!
This clever cuckoo has conned a mother wren into bringing it up in place of her own babies. Mom's the word!

BRAIN BOX

Orangutans sometimes use large leaves as umbrellas. They have even been seen to use leaves as napkins and "toilet paper."

Scientists have discovered that fish can tell the time, and they also have great memories, remembering things for up to three months.

Sea lions can remember tricks they learned ten years earlier. Trainers have taught sea lions that certain hand gestures have meaning, and they can understand a whole sentence of gestures, such as "fetch the large white ball."

Pigs have been trained to detect explosive mines in the field of war. Their trainers say they are better than dogs, because they are not only more intelligent, but also have a better sense of smell.

More than 1.5 million types, or species, of animal have been found so far—but scientists are still looking for the other 28.5 million they think exist. Why can't these eagle-eyed researchers find them? Well, many creatures are either masters of disguise, or hide from view to survive!

It's a dog-eat-dog world out there and these clever defenders blend in with their surroundings to avoid becoming lunch. It's a cunning trick known as camouflage—and many animals, especially insects, are experts.

Camouflage isn't all about defense. Prowling predators, like striped tigers and spotted leopards, disappear among the dappled shadows of their forest homes. Becoming invisible is a handy trick when you're a hungry hunter!

CHAMELEON

Male panther chameleons live on the island of Madagascar and are famous for their fabulous displays of color. Their skin can turn from red to blue or green in seconds. A sudden flush of color impresses the ladies!

THORN BUGS

Cunningly disguised as sharp thorns, these female thorn bugs suck sap from a tree. Any keen-sighted bird that sees through the camouflage and takes a bite will quickly discover that these fancy fakers taste foul.

KEY FACTS

→ Black, yellow, and red are nature's code for danger. Wearing stripes or spots in these colors can keep predators at bay, even if you're a totally harmless beastie.

→ It doesn't matter how cleverly camouflaged you are if you stink. That's why smelly animals aren't usually camouflaged.

→ Leaf-eating insects are so well disguised that there are maybe thousands of species that have never been spotted.

DANGER!

They may be yellow, but they're not cowards! Frightened yellow-bellied toads flip onto their backs, showing brightly colored undersides. The yellow warns predators: "Danger: poison!"

Upside down!

◎ **Chameleons** use their color-changing skills to scare off love rivals rather than as camouflage. They can also change color when the temperature or light changes, or they are unwell.

◎ **Cuttlefish** are eight-armed sea creatures that can send waves of shimmering color down their body, changing shades and patterns in seconds.

◎ **Stick insects** stay still and make like a twig. If their cunning disguise isn't working, they drop all their legs off for maximum effect. Luckily, the legs grow back!

◎ **Sleepy sloths** hang upside down in trees and snooze for 18 hours out of 24. Green plants grow in the sloths' fur, providing perfect camouflage in their rain forest homes.

LEAF INSECT

Leaf insects are one of nature's most extraordinary sights—if you ever get to see one, that is! This is Phyllium giganteum, the world's largest leaf insect, and it grows to more than 5 inches long.

where is it?

BARK MANTID

Don't challenge a bark mantid to a game of hide and go seek—unless you're happy to lose! They're quite common creatures in Australia, but you're only likely to see one if it's moving.

29

FAMILY MATTERS

GETTING TOGETHER

The multi-colored peacock is a bird that dresses to impress. He can fan out his tail, in an eye-opening display of shimmering colors and stunning patterns.

It's an ingenious tactic; a show-off with perfect plumage is more likely to attract the attention of the watching peahens. The females admire bright colors and large "eyespots" in the feathers—and the more eyespots the better! Once a female has chosen her favorite male she will mate with him, and soon starts laying eggs. The most marvelous males win over a number of females to mate with, while shabby-looking peacocks remain alone.

The Virginia opossum is the USA's only naturally occurring marsupial.

After about 100 days, the babies climb onto their mom's back to hitch a ride.

The newborns crawl straight into their mother's pouch to grow.

An opossum mom usually has 13 babies at once.

LIFE STORIES

The story of how an animal lives, from birth to death, is a life-cycle.

If an animal can find a healthy and strong mate it is more likely to have youngsters that will survive. Some animals make a big effort to impress those they like—to show how fit they are. This is called a courtship.

Mammals are animals that give birth to live young and feed them with milk. Usually it's the mom who provides the milk, but in the job-sharing world of Dayak fruit bats, it's a job for the dads too!

BIG WORD ALERT

REPRODUCTION
The way that an animal has young is called reproduction. Some animals can have young all by themselves, but it's more common to have two parents: a male and a female.

You said we were friends!
During mating, a female praying mantis usually gets the munchies and bites off her partner's head!

twist it!

A queen white ant, or termite, lays 30,000 eggs a day!

Snakes and lizards are reptiles and lay their eggs on land.

Amphibians, such as frogs and toads, have to lay their eggs in water.

Female rhinos spray smelly urine, and males will fight each other, sometimes to the death, to mate with them.

Sea horses are romantic, dancing for each other every day during the mating period. The female lays her eggs inside a special pouch on the male's body, and he takes care of them until they hatch.

TRUE LOVE

DADDY DAY-CARE
Male jawfish protect their eggs by keeping them inside their enormous mouths. Without their fatherly care, chances are that most of the eggs would be eaten before ever hatching.

NATURAL BORN KILLERS

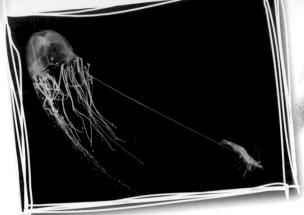

Imagine you are swimming in the beautiful clear waters of Australia when you feel something long and smooth glide over your leg. It's time to start counting: if you've been stung by a box jellyfish you've got about four minutes to live.

These animals, which are also known as sea wasps, are almost see-through and have long, trailing tentacles that are covered in rapid-fire stingers. If you haven't got any anti-venom tucked into your swimming suit you're in hot water! The poison from those stingers will give you excruciating pain, a burning feeling, and a one-way ticket to death.

Brown bears are dangerous, and do kill people!

STAY SAFE

- Animals normally kill people only if they are very hungry or scared.
- Humans are in the most danger from deadly creatures when they move into those animals' natural habitats.
- The most dangerous animal on the planet is the human—that's us! Unlike most other animals, we are able to destroy entire environments, and totally wipe out other species.

BIG KILLERS

Brazilian wandering spider: there are more than 30 types of deadly spider, but this feisty beast has a bad temper and attacks anyone and anything.

Black mamba: this skinny snake is a super-speedy assassin. It lurks in trees or crevices before attacking and can slither faster than you can run! Its deadly venom acts quickly, but kills slowly and painfully.

Cape buffalo: this curly-horned bruiser is the bully of the African plains. Get in its way, and one of these big beasts will run you down like a tank at full speed.

Golden poison-dart frog: don't touch this little fella, or you'll croak! Its highly poisonous skin can cause instant death.

Plasmodium: this tiny creature lives in the spit of mosquitoes and causes the deadly disease malaria. Malaria is spread when mosquitoes bite people, and is responsible for around one million human deaths every year in Africa alone.

The Brazilian wandering spider's venom causes unbelievable pain before death.

Ripley's...... Believe It or Not!®

One day, a Brazilian man found his six-year-old son in the jaws of an anaconda: that's an enormous South American snake. The poor boy had been nearly entirely swallowed. With no time to spare, the man picked up a wooden oar and smacked the snake with it, until it coughed the boy out. He was still alive!

Scott MacInnes is un-bear-ably unlucky. He lives in Alaska and has been attacked and savaged twice by brown bears. On the plus side, he did survive both attacks, despite major wounds.

Saltwater crocodiles don't kill people out of fear, but out of hunger. When a riverboat sank in Indonesia, in 1975, more than 40 passengers were set upon and eaten by saltwater crocs.

Ants are more deadly than they look. Bulldog ants and jumper ants inject painful acid into their prey, which can sometimes kill humans. There are rumors that columns of army ants and driver ants can climb all over a human victim, stinging and then eating them!

DEAD END

More people die from bee stings each year than from shark attacks or snake bites.

Gustave is a cold-blooded killer from Burundi. This giant African crocodile is rumored to have killed around 300 people.

Hippos kill more people in Africa than any other large animal. They are herbivores, but can attack humans to protect their calves and defend their territory.

Every year, 10,000 Indians lose their lives after being bitten by cobras.

One box jellyfish has enough venom to kill 60 people.

↑ TWIST IT! ↑

KILLING MACHINE

Saltwater crocodiles are the world's largest living reptiles, and unfortunately they've got big appetites, too. They are known as Australia's most dangerous animals.

SEE ME IN **ACTION** ON PAGE 23!

MEET THE UGLIES!

NATURE'S TOP 5

NAKED MOLE-RAT

Good looks don't matter to these burrowing mammals. They're nasty to look at, and nasty by nature: males kidnap youngsters from other colonies and keep them as slaves, forcing them to dig new tunnels.

JUDGES' COMMENTS

I almost lost my breakfast!

1st

GIANT SUNFISH

A giant sunfish starts life as small fry, but increases its weight 60 million times until adulthood—when it looks like a giant floating head and is the size of a car!

JUDGES' COMMENTS

Unspeakably ugly—looks like my old math teacher!!

2nd

4th

MARINE IGUANA

Ocean views and salty water don't suit any lizards—except the marine iguanas of the Galápagos Islands. These giant salt-covered sunbathers dive for food in the waters, or graze on seaweed in rocky pools nearby.

JUDGES' COMMENTS

Godzilla's ugly brother.

3rd

JUDGES' COMMENTS

We felt the nice haircut really sets off the big flappy nose!

PROBOSCIS MONKEY

You've got to feel sorry for this fella. If he looks up too quickly his giant schnoz will flop back and smack him in the eyes! His pot belly and big nose are a hit with the ladies though.

JUDGES' COMMENTS

Good effort, we particularly like the big spiky boil on the back of the neck.

THORNY DEVIL

This Australian lizard is no shrinking violet. It feeds during the day, relying on camouflage and its armory of spines to keep it safe. A thorny devil can eat 2,500 ants in one meal!

5th

ANIMAL TALK

Dolphins whistle to each other, chimps bang tree trunks like drums, and a honeybee shakes its rear end in a weird wiggle dance. Animals may not be able to talk like us, but they can certainly get their messages across.

Communication is crucial. If you can talk to your friends you can warn them when a predator is nearby, tell them where they can find food, or declare your love! Stick a few bright and bold stripes or spots on your skin and you could be telling predators to stay away because you taste vile, or have vicious venom up your sleeve.

WHISTLE

Dolphins call to each other by whistling. Amazingly, a group of dolphins gives each dolphin a name—which has its own special whistle.

RUMBLE

Elephants can communicate over many miles using very low rumbling sounds, which travel through the ground. Other elephants pick up these signals through their feet. This way, females can let adult males know they would be welcome to visit the herd!

WIGGLE

When a honeybee has found a good patch of flowers it flies back to the hive and starts dancing. By running up and down, and wiggling its body, the bee tells the others exactly where to find the flowers!

YOU LOOKING AT ME?

SHRIEK

When a chimpanzee shrieks, he is telling the rest of the gang that he's found food. Chimps also use their faces to show emotions such as anger and playfulness.

The bold colors on a male mandrill's face tell other members of his troop just how strong and important he is. When he bares his enormous teeth he's saying, "Don't mess with me!"

QUICK, SCRAM!

Gunnison's prairie dogs are smarter than they look. With one call they warn their friends of an impending hawk attack—and the group looks up before scattering. A different call signals "coyote" and the gang make for the safety of their burrows.

UNW-LCOME GUESTS

PARASITES

Welcome to the world of the meanest, most selfish of all creatures—the pathetic parasites. These lazy lowlife take their food directly from other, living animals—often hurting them.

Once settled upon, or inside, another animal (called the host), pesky parasites have got an easy life, absorbing food and making a comfortable home for themselves. The problem comes when it's time to reproduce. Getting eggs or babies from one host to another can be a challenge, especially if home is someone's gut, liver, or even brain. Despite those difficulties, there are parasites aplenty out there, mostly invisible to our eyes.

The body swells with blood.

A female louse can lay up to 300 eggs

A human body louse feeds on human blood.

Bed fellows

Dust mites join you in your bed at night, but don't complain. These little creatures munch their way through all your dead skin cells. You could count about two million of them in one bed! Bed bugs, however, are not such helpful bedfellows: they feed on human blood!

Ripley's
Believe It or Not!®

That's disgusting!

The larvae of the botfly burrow into live flesh and eat it. They often attack horses but can target humans. Aaron Dallas had five botfly larvae removed from his head, where he could hear and feel them moving around.

BIG
WORD ALERT

INVERTEBRATE

Many parasites are invertebrates—that is animals without backbones, such as worms and fleas.

The candiru is a parasitic fish of the Amazon. It swims up a person's penis and settles down in the bladder, where pee, or urine, is stored. The poor host will need surgery soon, or face death.

Sinus flukes (similar to leeches) burrow into the brains of whales.

One of the most dangerous parasites in the world is a rat flea that carries bubonic plague. This is a disease that was common long ago, and caused around 25 million human deaths in Europe alone.

Roundworms, or nematodes, are some of the most abundant animals on the planet. There are more than 20,000 species and many of them are parasites, living in the guts of other animals.

A cat flea can leap over 13 inches. That's like a human jumping to the top of a skyscraper in a single leap. Fleas can also keep jumping for days without taking a break.

twist it!

Eaten from the inside out!

Parasitic wasps make sure their babies have plenty to eat, by laying their eggs inside, or on, a caterpillar's body! When the eggs hatch, the tiny larvae don't have to bother searching for fresh food.

TERRIBLE TICKS!

BEFORE

AFTER

Ticks suck up so much blood that their bodies fill up like a balloon. They can't fly or jump, but they carry many diseases that are deadly to humans.

The wasp lays its eggs all over the poor caterpillar.

Vile!

This putrid sight is actually lice feeding on the skin of a giant grey whale.

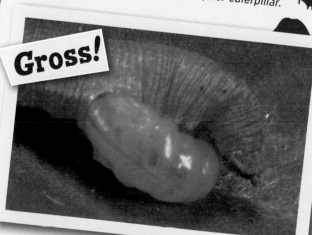

Gross!

After eating the caterpillar's guts and juices, a wasp larva bursts out of its skin!

SWARM!
SAFETY IN NUMBERS

Desert locusts are loners, until they run out of food. Then, their brains produce a special friendship chemical called seratonin.

The locusts get an urge to hang out together—often in their billions! The giant gang then guzzles its way through millions of tons of food.

When a bunch of animals all get together they are called a swarm. Swarming happens because there is safety in numbers. When birds or fish gather in their thousands they buddy-up like one mighty monster. Each animal copies what its neighbor is doing, and the giant mass of moving flesh is more than a match for most predators.

KEY FACTS

- The time of year, the season, and weather conditions can all play a part in swarming behavior.

- Swarming is a good idea if lots of your favorite food is ripe and ready to eat for just a short time. You can gobble it all up!

- Some swarms have bosses. These leaders communicate with the rest of the gang, telling them where to go and what to do.

BIRDS OF A FEATHER FLOCK TOGETHER

Never was that more true than in the case of red-billed queleas. These seed-eating African birds number more than half a billion, and one flock can hold hundreds of millions of birds. When they settle on trees to strip off the fruit, the queleas' combined weight can break branches.

IT'S A STING THING

Giant swarms of stinging jellyfish, like these thimble jellyfish, are bad news for swimmers. They are becoming more common as oceans warm up.

Dr. Norman Gary is an insect scientist who tours the world with his Thriller Bee Show. While he plays the "bee flat" clarinet as many as 100,000 bees swarm all over him, even entering his mouth. Dr Gary is a bee expert who has written hundreds of scientific papers on his favorite subject, and has even trained bees to act in movies.

BEE FLAT

Locusts in a feeding frenzy can cause terrible food shortages and misery for humans as they strip crops bare.

twist it!

ONE AND ALL

Millions of salmon-pink flamingos gather at Lake Nakuru in Kenya to feed on the bacteria that live in the water. The birds get their pink color from their food.

King penguins can live together in enormous groups that number 600,000 or more.

In 1981, a swarm of 10 million krill, which are shrimp-like creatures that live in the ocean, collected near Antarctica. There were so many of them, the swarm could be seen from space! It was the largest swarm of any animal that has ever been known.

Periodical cicadas are bugs that survive for 17 years underground, then all emerge at the same time to breed. Males have a drum-like part of the body, which can be used to create a loud noise, to impress the females. When millions of cicadas swarm, the noise is so loud it's painful to the human ear.

Killer bees were created when scientists got different types of honeybees to mate. Twenty-six of the new, ferocious type of bee escaped from the laboratory and 40 years later had become established in the wild, creating enormous swarms. Although each sting is no worse than an ordinary bee sting, the killer insects are much more aggressive and likely to sting in large numbers, which can prove deadly.

BEAST BUDDIES

BAILEY THE BUFFALO

Bailey the buffalo is not just a pet, he's treated like one of the family and is allowed to watch TV. He even eats at the kitchen table!

LION LOVER

Animal scientist Kevin Richardson loves lions, and is happy to cuddle up with them. He reckons it's easy to be friends with a lion, as long as you hang out with them while they are still cubs.

THE COBRA KING

King cobras are one of the world's most deadly snakes, but the Thai people of King Cobra Village keep them close to their hearts, literally! Most households keep a live cobra in a wooden box beneath their home, and get it out once a year for the village's three-day snake festival, when men fight the snakes and women dance with them.

HOTEL TRUNKS

Elephants are creatures of habit, and not particularly frightened of people. So they weren't bothered when a hotel was built across their route to some mango trees. Now hotel staff and guests stand back and watch while the elephants march through the hotel lobby to get to the ripe fruits!

THERE'S A HIPPO IN THE HOUSE!

How would you feel about adopting a wild animal? That's what a South African couple did when they found a newborn hippo, stranded and orphaned by floods. They named the cute little baby Jessica, and cared for her in their home while she grew, and grew, and GREW! Adult hippos weigh up to 3.5 tons, and can reach over 11 feet long, so Jessica had to leave home, and move in with a group of wild hippos that lived nearby!

WOLF MAN

Shaun Ellis is so comfortable in the company of wolves that he knows how to interact with them. He has studied their body language, facial expressions, and eating habits for years.

GOING, GOING, GONE

EVOLUTION AND EXTINCTION

One quarter of all mammals and one third of all amphibians (frogs, newts, and toads) are threatened with extinction, partly because humans are destroying animal habitats faster than ever before.

When people turn forests into farms or towns, and pollute natural environments, like the oceans and rivers, more and more animals die. Some species are killed for their skins and body parts, which are used in some traditional remedies. Other creatures are simply hunted for food or collected as pets.

LONESOME GEORGE

BIG WORD ALERT

EXTINCT
When every last animal of a species has died, it has become extinct. Dinosaurs, dodos, and extinct carrier pigeons are all extinct.

GIANT TORTOISE

GHARIAL

10 of the most endangered species

Scientists believe Lonesome George is the last of his kind: a type of GIANT TORTOISE from the Galapagos Islands. When George dies, so will his species.

In the last ten years, the number of GHARIALS has halved, plummeting to just 200 or so. These fish-eating crocodiles live in India and Nepal. They were once hunted for their skins, but are now critically endangered because their river habitats are being destroyed by humans.

All rhinos are in danger of extinction, but there are only about 50 JAVAN RHINOS left. Once there were thousands of these grass-grazers in Southeast Asia, but nearly all of them have been killed for their horns.

There are just 90 KAKAPOS left, and they are looked after by a group of scientists. Kakapos are the world's biggest parrots, and longest-living birds. They can't fly, which is why they nearly died out when people brought predators to their New Zealand home.

Gorillas are peaceful, plant-eating apes that live in African forests. All gorillas are endangered, but CROSS RIVER GORILLAS are especially rare because farms and roads are destroying their habitats. There are about 250 to 300 left.

The IBERIAN LYNX will probably be the first big cat to become extinct for at least 2,000 years. There are no more than 38 adult females left in the wild,

SPIDER, was discovered, but there are only a few hundred of these eight-legged creatures, and they live in a handful of plantations on an island near India.

SUMATRAN TIGERS are poisoned, hunted, trapped, and snared, and now there are less than 400 left in the wild. Also, the forests where they live are being turned into farms.

All over the world, the GIANT PANDA is used as a symbol for saving animals. There are about 1,600 pandas in the wild and they mostly eat bamboo. A panda baby is 1/900th the size of its mother, making it one of the smallest mammal babies.

A SOUTHERN BLUEFIN TUNA can live for 40 years and reach over 6 feet in length, if it doesn't get caught and eaten first. So many have been killed for food that they are now in serious danger of becoming extinct.

GIANT PANDA

JAVAN RHINO

CROSS RIVER GORILLA

SOUTHERN BLUEFIN TUNA

SUMATRAN TIGER

INDEX

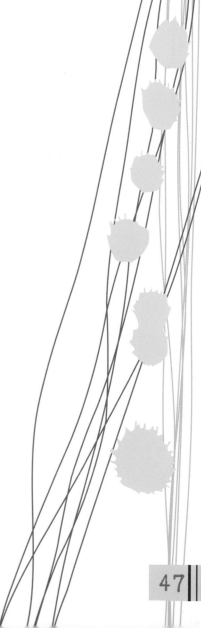

ACKNOWLEDGMENTS

COVER (l) Matt Rourke/AP/PA Photos, (r) © Gabriela Staebler/zefa/Corbis; **2** (c) © Olga Khoroshunova – fotolia.com, (b) Courtesy of Janice Wolf; **3** (t) © Eric Isselée – istockphoto.com, (r) Linda Cowen/Wolfpack Management; **4** © Gabriela Staebler/zefa/Corbis; **5** (t/r) Matt Rourke/AP/PA Photos; **6** © Tobias Bernhard/zefa/Corbis; **7** (t) NHPA/Photoshot, (c) Used by permission of Rodney Fox, (b/r) © Oceans Image/Photoshot, (b) © Jeffrey L. Rotman/Corbis; **8** (sp) Neil Bromhall/www.photolibrary.com; **9** (t/l, b/l) Peter Scoones/Science Photo Library, (r) © Olga Khoroshunova – fotolia.com, (b/r) Gregory Ochocki/Science Photo Library; **10** © NHPA/Photoshot; **11** (c) © ktsdesign – fotolia.com, (t) Adrian Bicker/Science Photo Library, (r) © NHPA/Photoshot; **12** © Shusuke Sezai/epa/Corbis, (r) Oceans-Image/Photoshot; **13** (t/l) Karl H. Switak/Science Photo Library, (t/r) Tom McHugh/Science Photo Library, (b) © Larry Williams/Corbis; **14** (t) © N & B – fotolia.com, (b) © NHPA/Photoshot; **14–15** (l) Courtesy of Janice Wolf; **15** (c) Ministry of Fisheries via Getty Images, (b, r) © NHPA/Photoshot; **16–17** Jim Zipp/Science Photo Library; **17** (r) © NHPA/Photoshot, (t) Rexford Lord/Science Photo Library, (b) Eric Gay/AP/PA Photos; **18** (b) © Eric Isselée – istockphoto.com, (sp) © Remi Benali/Corbis; **19** (l) © filip put – istockphoto.com, (r) Reuters/Ho New; **20** © DLILLC/Corbis; **20–21** (b) © N & B – fotolia.com; **21** (t) © Anthony Bannister/Gallo Images/Corbis, (b) Andy Rouse/Rex Features; **22** (b/l) © John Anderson – fotolia.com, (sp) David B Fleetham/www.photolibrary.com, (t, t/r) © NHPA/Photoshot; **23** (t/c/l, t/c/r, t/r) © NHPA/Photoshot, (b) © Roger Garwood & Trish Ainslie/Corbis; **24** Eye Of Science/Science Photo Library; **25** (bgd) George Bernard/Science Photo Library (t/l) Mark Fairhurst/UPPA/Photoshot, (b/l) Cheryl Power/Science Photo Library, (t/c) Eye Of Science/Science Photo Library, (t/r) Alan Sirulnikoff/Science Photo Library, (b/r) Pasieka/Science Photo Library; **26** Manoj Shah/Getty Images; **27** (t/l) © Paul Stock – fotolia.com, (t/c, t/r) Satoshi Kuribayashi/www.photolibrary.com, (c) Bournemouth News/Rex Features, (b/r) Maurice Tibbles/www.photolibrary.com; **28** (l) © NHPA/Photoshot, (r) © sunset man – fotolia.com; **29** (l, r, t, t/c) © NHPA/Photoshot; **30** (t) © Eky Chan – fotolia.com, (r) Frank Lukasseck/Getty Images; **31** (t, b) © NHPA/Photoshot; **32** (l) James Balog/Imagebank/Getty Images, (b) © Yaroslav Gnatuk – fotolia.com, (t) David Doubilet/National Geographic/Getty Images; **33** (t) © Holger Mette – fotolia.com, (b) © NHPA/Photoshot; **34** (b) Mark Newman/FLPA, (t) Hiroya Minakuchi/Minden Pictures/FLPA; **35** (l) © NHPA/Photoshot, (b/r) Michael K. Nichols/National Geographic/Getty Images, (t) John Beatty/Science Photo Library; **36** (l) © Kitch Bain – fotolia.com, (c) © Karen Roach – fotolia.com, (b/l) © The physicist – fotolia.com; **37** (t/l) Michael Nichols/National Geographic/Getty Images, (c) Gail Shumway/Taxi/Getty Images, (r) © RebeccaAnne – fotolia.com; **38** (l) © NHPA/Photoshot, (r) Darlyne A. Murawski/National Geographic/Getty Images; **39** (l) © Dwight Davis – fotolia.com, (b/l) Ken Lucas/Getty Images, (c) © Heinz Waldukat – fotolia.com, (t) © Henrik Larsson – fotolia.com, (c/r) © Stephen Bonk – fotolia.com, (b/r) Robert F. Sisson/National Geographic/Getty Images; **40** (l) Oceans-Image/Photoshot, (r) Bildagentur RM/www.photolibrary.com; **40–41** (bgd) David Shale/www.photolibrary.com; **41** (t/r) Sipa Press/Rex Features; **42** (l) Carlo Allegri/Getty Images, (b) Photograph by Falise Thierry/Gamma/Eyedea/Camera Press London, (c) Zoom/Barcroft Media; **43** (t/l, r) Zoom/Barcroft Media, (b) Linda Cowen/Wolfpack Management; **44** (l) © siloto – fotolia.com, (c) Reuters/Guillermo Granja; **45** (t/l) Tony Camacho/Science Photo Library, (l) Sue Flood/Getty Images, (b/r) © Timothy Lubcke – fotolia.com, (c/r) © ImagineImages – fotolia.com, (t/r) © dzain – fotolia.com

Key: t = top, b = bottom, c = center, l = left, r = right, sp = single page, dp = double page, bgd = background

Every attempt has been made to acknowledge correctly and contact copyright holders and we apologize in advance for any unintentional errors or omissions, which will be corrected in future editions.

Elsmere Library
30 Spruce Avenue
Wilmington, DE 19805

J
590   BC#33910045534956 $19.95
D   De la Bedoyere, Camilla
            Wild animals

                    els
                  05/14/12

NO LONGER THE
PROPERTY OF
NEW CASTLE COUNTY